HOW TO ACHIEVE
SUCCESSFUL
MIGRATION AND
INTEGRATION

Turning what could have been threats and weaknesses to opportunities and strengths

WORKBOOK

EPHRAIM OSAGHAE MBL, PMP, MBA

NOTE | This book is intended to be a workbook. However, since you may be unable to write on electronic readers, you will need to do your reflections and associated writing on paper, computer or other writing devices.

TABLE OF CONTENT

INTRODUCTION

The focus of this workbook is to provide practical information and wisdom for getting the best value out of the investments in the big move of migration, relocation, and integration. The guidance provided is largely based on lived experiences of immigrants that have worked the path. It is not about how to migrate, though the author can provide such information of a general nature. He works in partnership with certified migration agents, where applicable - as part of his holistic support for his clients.

The key aspects of migration value chain are covered in this workbook. They include factors to consider as part of pre-migration preparations, setting SMART goals, and settling well into your new location. Readers and users will learn and receive guidance based on real stories of real people that should lead to real actions for success. The ultimate aim is to help intending and new immigrants with a reflective guide that will help them to proactively elicit and document key actions to be taken in adopting, adapting and achieving their goals for the big move. Settled immigrants can also use this workbook, it is never too late to achieve your success.

This is a workbook, which means it helps you to reflect and take action after learning what you need to do in response to each of the principles and steps presented in this book. The best way to get the maximum value is to use it alongside reading the author's two books: (1) A Handbook for Migrants: The Good, The Challenges and The Lessons and (2) Adopt Adapt Achieve: An Amazing Triple A Guide for Successful Relocation, Change and Integration. Users of this workbook should not hold back when doing the reflective writing aspect in the spaces provided. It is better to have more texts initially which you can fine-tune over time as you use this valuable tool during an individual or group workshop sessions.

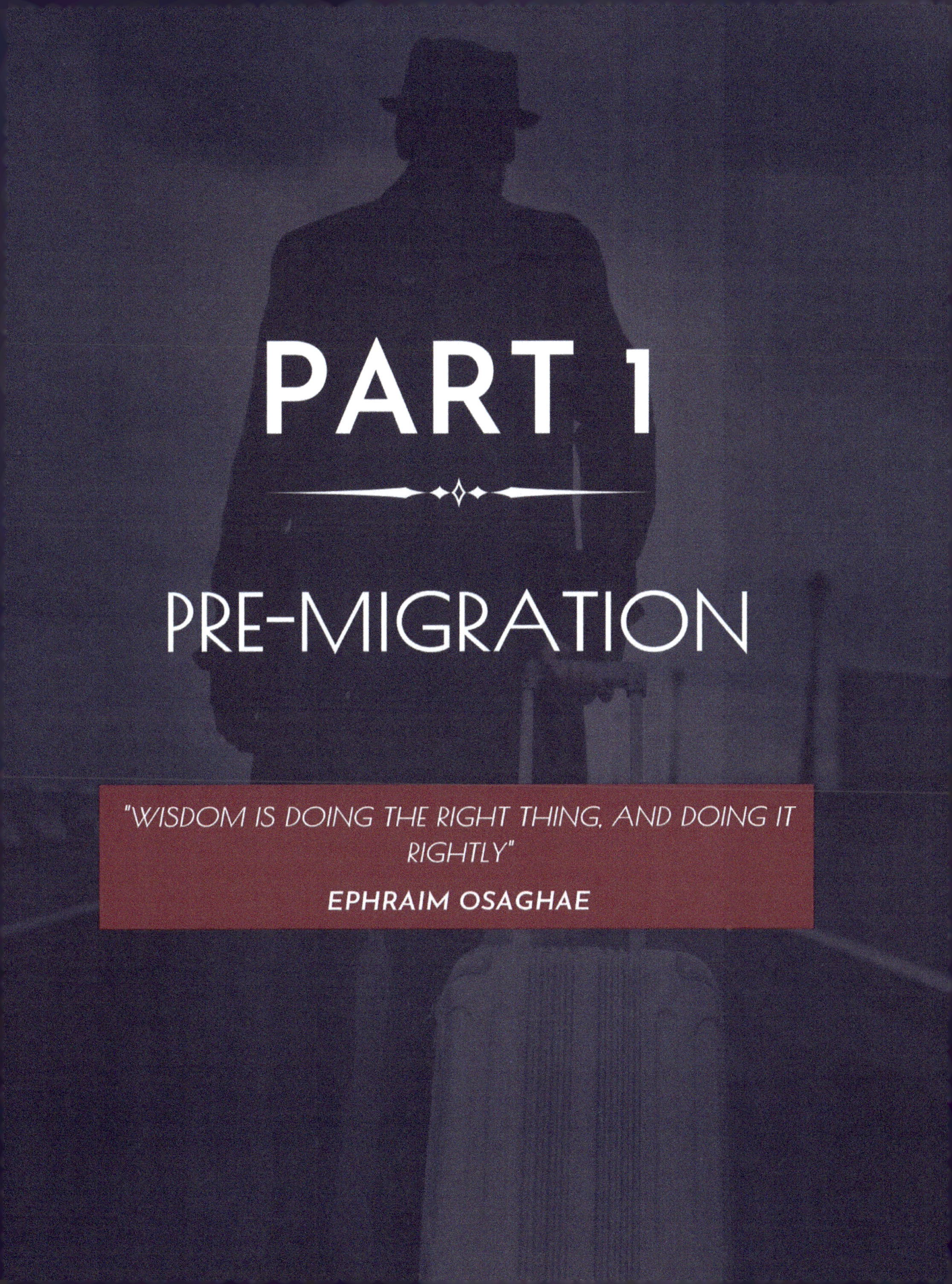

PART 1

PRE-MIGRATION

"WISDOM IS DOING THE RIGHT THING, AND DOING IT RIGHTLY"

EPHRAIM OSAGHAE

01   YOUR STORY

> "Your story is part of your competitive advantages: articulate it, cherish it, harness it" *Ephraim Osaghae*

I have a story worth sharing. Everyone has a story they can share as well. Your story states your identity. It expresses your uniqueness and your unique journey, or episodes thereof. It conveys your value and your spread. It constitutes part of your competitive advantages in life.

Migration or relocation is a big move! While acknowledging the significance of the change, it should not stop or shut-down our stories. Rather, it should add to the length, the breadth, and the overall richness. Our stories are dynamic. Writing your storyboard is one way to envision the future and success you want which in this context, will include the significant change of emigration.

It is important for you to tell your story yourself or at least, ensure that it is correctly told if another person or agency tells it for you. Articulate and document your story as early as you can, preferably long before you even decide to relocate. It may be sketchy initially, but it will only get clearer and more robust with time, experience and intentionality.

REFLECTIONS:

- What is your story now?

- How will your story change as a result of relocation (VISION)?

- To what greater good will you use your story (MORE IMPACT)?

02 THE DECISION TO MIGRATE (START WITH THE *WHYS*)

> "Choices are the hinges of destiny" *Edwin Markham*

It is critical to settle the *Whys* of migrating. It will help to set right expectations even before the move. It will also motivate you to seek reliable information about the new country of destination.

Your *Whys* would enhance your stability during tough times in the new location. Indeed, challenging times will come in different aspects of life. It will provide you with a reference anchor for responding to changes in a more definite and proactive manner. It will also afford you the basis for decision making during periods of uncertainties. It would enhance your capacity for resilience and adaptability, where applicable.

Relocating from one country to another is a life changing journey that can define the success or failure of one's life goals especially if one does not have adequate information regarding the new location. Unfortunately, it is almost impossible to get that information until you've already migrated. This workbook is helping to bridge that gap.

WHY?

REFLECTIONS:

○ Why do you want to migrate?

○ What do you know about the new country / location? What should you know?

○ How do you find reliable information for proactive decision-making and actions?

03 SMART GOALS

> "SMART goals are smart indeed" *Ephraim Osaghae*

It is important to undertake a reflective exercise to set your migration goals well ahead of relocation. Often, people take this aspect for granted - to their disadvantages. There should be intentionality in being smart in setting your goals starting from determining your big WHY as mentioned in an earlier section of this workbook. While this workbook is primarily focused on the goal of migration and integration in general, the principles are applicable to other components of the relocation context. These include studying, family, career, business, investment, holidaying, and ageing.

It is even more important for your migration goals to be SMART - Specific, Measurable, Achievable, Realistic, and Time-bound. It is worth the time and efforts considering the significance of the hope, investments and change associated with relocation. Setting these goals may be challenging for some people especially for migration-related matters. This is where the use of an experienced facilitator will be helpful. The value you place on the success of your migration is an incentive to do it, and do it rightly.

"I recommend that you focus on both substance and process of your goals. I believe that both are equally important: by setting a high-quality SMART goal you will enable yourself to be conscious and your actions will carry more meaning; meanwhile, it is the execution of the SMART goals strategy that separates achievers from the rest of the people." *Anna Stevens*

REFLECTIONS:

- How SMART are your emigration / relocation goals?

- Have you checked your goals recently for SMARTness? What needs to be updated?

- Are you working with an accountability coach to help you achieve your goals?

PART 2

---◆---

TRANSITIONING & SETTLING WELL IN THE NEW LOCATION

"I KNOW THE TASK AHEAD SEEMS IMPOSSIBLE, BUT ALL WE NEED TO DO IS BEGIN . . .
A JOURNEY OF A THOUSAND MILES STARTS WITH A SINGLE STEP"

JENNIFER DONNELLY

04 PREPARE, PREPARE, PREPARE

> "Prepare, prepare, and keep preparing . . . as if your success depends on your preparations. More often, it does" *Edwin Markham*

Preparations require time and efforts including researching and finding as much facts as you can about the new country where you will be residing shortly. This is a big move! It is not a short holiday trip and in many cases, it is a permanent relocation unless you still retain that option to go back to your country of origin.

Thus, you will give yourself the best shot at success in the new country or location if you invest the time, efforts and networks to know as much as you can well ahead of getting on the flight. The value of information in this context will provide you with a higher chance of success for better settlement and integration.

REFLECTIONS:

- What is the weather of the country like including the different seasons?

- What is the economy like and how easy is it to get a job and settle down?

- What is the diversity of people, food and cultures and the language/s for communication?

- What do you need to do now (before you leave your country of origin) to give yourself (and your family, where applicable) the best chance for success?

05 SETTLING-IN & INTEGRATION: USE SUPPORT NETWORKS

> "It is important to integrate while preserving and celebrating your identity and uniqueness" *Ephraim Osaghae*

New migrants often do it the hard way during the transitioning and settling into the new country or location. Many times, there is even no one to receive them at the airport, neither is anyone dedicated to providing guidance during those first critical few days or weeks of navigating their ways in such new terrains and experiences. It pays to maximize the use of established networks or close relatives already living in your target new country of residence, where available. It pays to be informed about the weather conditions and seasons, welcomed at the airport, shown the way around including undertaking the required documentation, how to use the transportation system, where to find schools, shops, etc. It may save you a lot of time and possibly, some costs as well.

However, many newcomers will not be disappointed when they arrive in a country with significantly more economic and infrastructural advancement than their home countries. This is especially the case if higher standard of living was part of the *Whys* for migrating. There would great network of roads with clear evidence of planned and actual maintenance. The utility will be seamlessly regular. Water, gas, electricity and internet will be constant for weeks and months without disruptions. Hospitals will not only be affordable (or even free in some cases), medical care will be of the highest standard in relative terms to the not-too-past experiences of the new migrant.

REFLECTIONS:

- Do you have relatives or friends in the new location that can provide you with support as part of your transitioning? If yes, list their names, contact details, etc.

- If the answer to the above question is no, can you secure the support of friends of relatives, friends of friends, etc.? If yes, list their names, contact details, etc.

- If the answers to the above two questions are negative, how do you bridge the gap i.e. the need for a support network to help you settle in and integrate into life in the new location?

06 DEALING WITH CULTURE SHOCKS

> "Culture shock is often felt sharply at the borders between countries, but sometimes it doesn't hit fully until you've been in a place for a long time" *Henri Cartier-Bresson*

The initial culture shock in settling down into the new country will be more apparent in some aspects of everyday living than others. One of them could be side of driving your car may be different from that of your home country.

Another one is family dynamics. For example, you may not have as much close family networks in the new country. Lastly, for the purpose of this workbook, there will be challenges with differences like accents, greeting styles, time management, etc.

The newcomer will need to adjust accordingly. However, the author advocates the right balance of adjustments while preserving one's uniqueness as a competitive advantage. It is about what to adopt, how to adapt, and achieving your goals.

REFLECTIONS:

● What are the potential culture shocks that you are likely to experience in your potential new location? The output from the reflective exercise of section #2 (Decision to Migrate) can be input here.

● What do you think about this quote by Clyde Kluckhon: "Every human is like all other humans, some other humans, and no other human"? How would you use the insights from your reflection to deal with culture shocks you may experience in the new location?

● Which cultural practices in your country of upbringing do you think you will need to change or retain as part of your integration in the new country or location?

PART 3

ADOPT ADAPT ACHIEVE: A TRIPLE-A GUIDE TO SUCCESS

"ENJOYING SUCCESS REQUIRES THE ABILITY TO ADAPT. ONLY BY BEING OPEN TO CHANGE WILL YOU HAVE A TRUE OPPORTUNITY TO GET THE MOST FROM YOUR TALENT"

NOLAN RYAN

"THE MEASURE OF INTELLIGENCE IS THE ABILITY TO CHANGE"

ALBERT EISTEIN

This section of the workbook provides hands-on intelligence on how to adopt the new country and key aspects thereof, how to adapt to changes that will definitely happen, and how to successfully achieve your goals. Career goals and the widely acknowledged SWOT analysis will be used for illustration. The principles apply to settling into a new life in many countries in the western world.

07 | OPPORTUNITIES

FACTORS IN THE ENVIRONMENT THAT COULD BE EXPLOITED FOR YOUR CAREER

> "A wise man will make more opportunities than he finds" *Francis Bacon*

Many countries in the western world offer direct and indirect opportunities for newcomers including enabling factors like stable economy, world-class infrastructure, and high standard of living. There are typically strong fiscal discipline and governance at all levels of government. Other attractive factors relate to dependable and affordable medical care, world-class transportation system, affordable high-quality education, social welfare, and security. Such stability has resulted in sustainable growth in various industries including pipeline of ongoing and scheduled projects that offer opportunities for employment and financial growth.

Most immigrants eagerly exploit such opportunities for financial wellbeing for themselves and their families while contributing to the growth of the economy of the host countries. They also enjoy the added advantages of exploring opportunities back in their homelands that they could tap into while living in the west. They have the edge of enjoying from both worlds as well as contributing to the economic and cultural growth of both as well. Harness and maximise this advantage!

REMARKS AND GUIDANCE ON HOW TO ADOPT & ADAPT

A stable economy, world-class infrastructure and high standard of living are some of the reasons (the WHYs) for people to emigrate even when they have reasonably good jobs back in their homelands. They consider longer-term prospects, overall stability and security for themselves and their families. Unfortunately, many have lacked these types of economic enablers back in their home countries.

Immigrants should adopt these undeniable benefits and associated stability for growth while also exploring opportunities back in their homelands. They can be the 'bridge' between investors and employers in the west and opportunities back in their homelands. They can exploit the advantages of knowing and living in multiple worlds.

REFLECTIONS:

- What are the opportunities in the new location that you aim to exploit? What's the plan?

- What are the opportunities in your home country that you can exploit? What's the plan?

08 STRENGTHS

CHARACTERISTICS OF YOUR CAREER THAT GIVE YOU AN ADVANTAGE OVER OTHERS

"We acquire the strength we have overcome" *Ralph Waldo Emerson*

Immigrants bring so much strength to their new countries of residence in the aspect of careers. They bring skills and value to businesses. It is widely acknowledged that cultural diversity contributes to creativity in the workplace. Hopefully, employers, leaders and team members recognize, value, use, celebrate and give credit accordingly.

Recent data have shown that some organisations would have to look beyond the Western world for new opportunities to remain viable. Thus, proactive immigrants are the best candidates that these companies would need for bridging these gaps. Immigrants are mostly multinational, multicultural, and resilient. They know the terrains in and around their homelands, countries of birth and upbringing. They may not necessarily have the high-worth networks for businesses, but they present as the best candidates for resilience. After all, it was their backyards! Arts, Sports, Resource and Culture industries are some of the areas with opportunities that immigrants could present as competitive candidates for jobs and investments facilitators.

REMARKS AND GUIDANCE ON HOW TO ADOPT & ADAPT

The strengths that immigrants bring into their new countries are needful and undeniable.

Articulate yours as an immigrant! Build, refine, and stretch them as required. You can also propose to employers the options of exploring opportunities back in your homeland even when they seemed not to be initially interested.

Be proactive by developing key leads before relocation and maintain contact with them as you settle into your new places. They could help your career.

REFLECTIONS:

- What would you consider to be your major strengths in career and other endeavours? What's the plan?

- Can you document and maintain viable contact with 5 key members of your current professional network that could play significant role/s in your career in the new location?

09 WEAKNESSES

CHARACTERISTICS THAT PUT YOU AT A DISADVANTAGE RELATIVE TO OTHERS

> "Try to look at your weakness and convert it into your strength"
> *ZigZiglar*

9.1 LANGUAGE AND COMMUNICATION

Limited English language skills are particularly challenging for immigrants from non-English speaking countries. They would need to spend months to learn to speak, read and write in English. More often, newcomers go through the ordeal of being made to pass English tests (e.g. IELTS) before they are considered for studies, employment, residency, and even citizenship. Many have been known to get stuck in this situation for a long time and it could be very frustrating. People and families from countries where English is the official language also face the same barrier as they are classified as non-English speaking since English is not the native language in their home countries.

In reality, there are cases where locals and immigrants struggle to understand each others even when they are speaking English. Communication styles, accents, voice tones, body language, etc., are different in many instances. This becomes a weakness for many new immigrants especially when they seek employment, studying, running businesses, etc.

REMARKS AND GUIDANCE ON HOW TO ADOPT & ADAPT

There are no easy solutions for language and communication barriers. Immigrants would have to adopt applicable languages in the new location. This may require learning, practising and communicating in the language until mastery. The other aspects like differences inaccent and voice tone will mostly get better with time.

Immigrants should mix-up with locals as much as reasonably practicable as part of the settlement process. This would help in fast-tracking communication and integration. The quicker you get beyond the frustrations of feeling that it is unfair to be made to learn the language that you have always spoken right from birth, the better you will overcome this barrier and get on with other aspects of your life in the new location.

REFLECTIONS:

- If you are yet to relocate: what can you do now to turn this weakness into strength?

- Already in the new location: what can you do now to turn this weakness into strength?

9.2 ACADEMIC AND PROFESSIONAL QUALIFICATIONS

The lack of recognition of hard-earned qualifications is another barrier to consider. Certificates of immigrants are being made redundant causing them to be 'flushed down the drain' at an alarming rate. This is irrespective of the fact that these qualifications would have been reviewed and verified by relevant professional bodies in the host countries as part of the skilled migration process, where applicable.

Many employers in the Western world place more weight on practical work experiences than academic qualifications. This is the case for Australia. Even in roles where academic qualifications are typically required like lecturing or researching in schools, they would value qualifications that are earned locally than those from overseas.

Whilst some potential employers will go the extra mile of requesting checks via the relevant professional bodies, others will hardly review the application from the immigrant with overseas qualification/s. This constitutes a weakness for immigrants especially with matters relating to employment and career growth.

REMARKS AND GUIDANCE ON HOW TO ADOPT & ADAPT

For intending, new and emerging immigrants: Firstly, accept the reality that there is no guarantee that you will use your qualifications even as a skilled visa holder. Secondly, be willing to be adaptable including acquiring relevant trade and short courses that may eventually secure a job for you. Lastly, ensure you are informed about the qualifications of demand well ahead of your arrival. Check the Country's approved list of skilled occupations as they change regularly. As part of your settling in the new location: be proactive in filling identified gaps even while you are working survival jobs in the meantime. Never give up on your goals even if it takes a few more steps to achieve them.

REFLECTIONS:

○ If you are yet to relocate: what can you do now to turn this weakness into strength?

○ Already in the new location: what can you do now to turn this weakness into strength?

9.3   WORK EXPERIENCE

Immigrants face a dilemma when it comes to the challenges with local work experience as a requirement for employment. This can be likened to the classic "chicken and egg" analogy: how do you get the experience without employment? They end up missing out for many years as they struggle to secure opportunities with local companies that will give them a chance even for non-paying, short-term volunteering roles in a bid to acquire local experience.

Previous work experiences back in their home countries are sometimes also relegated by potential employers. The common reasons are that these non-local experiences are not compliant with local systems and/or they cannot be validated. While this is understandable for some disciplines and industries like law, defence, immigration, etc., but one would have thought that engineering skills and experiences in an industry like manufacturing, mining, or oil and gas, will be mostly transferable.

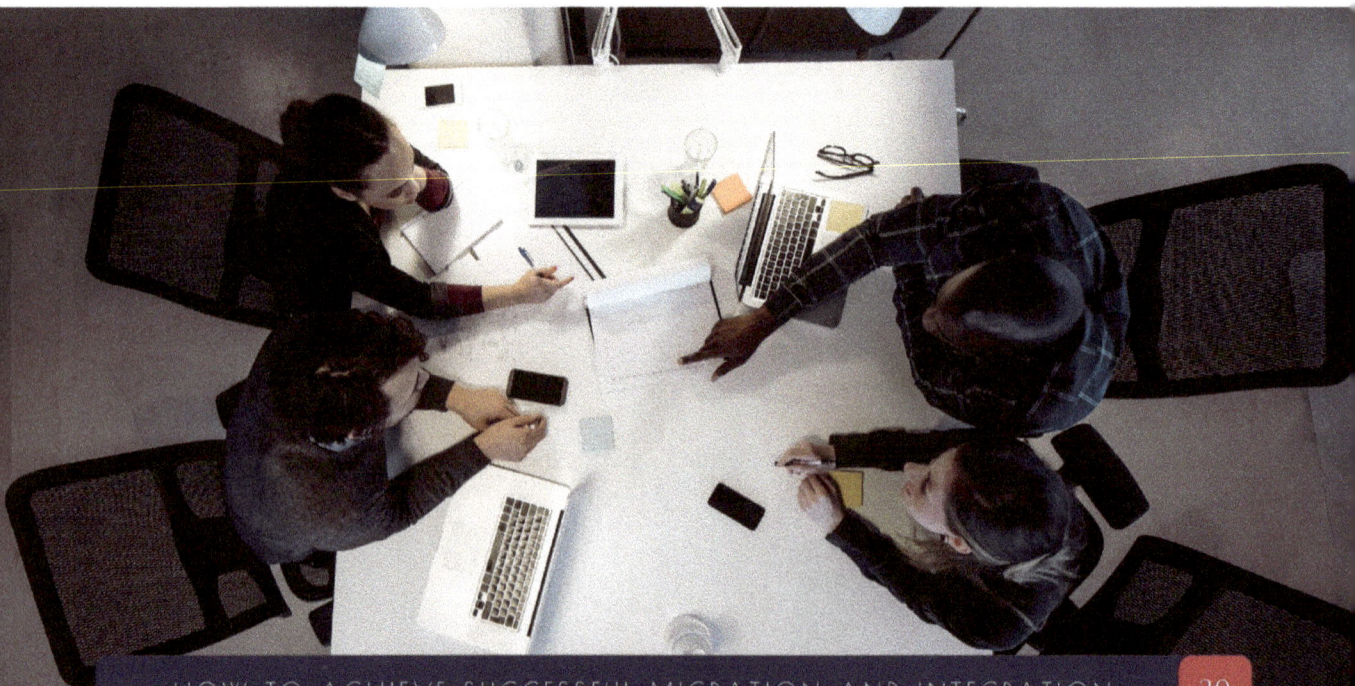

REMARKS AND GUIDANCE ON HOW TO ADOPT & ADAPT

This situation with work experience is the reality on ground in most countries in the west. Arguably, governments and employing organisations have their pre-set strategies and demands in terms of the regions they want the newcomers to relocate to, industries and professions they want them to work in, types of training and qualifications required, etc.

Immigrants can be proactive in accessing this information and being guided accordingly. The more you are aligned to these local aspirations, the easier and faster you will secure employment and/or business opportunities. Such information will help you to prepare better for the relocation, targeting work and volunteering experiences, and integration.

REFLECTIONS:

- If you are yet to relocate: what can you do now to turn this weakness into strength?

- Already in the new location: what can you do now to turn this weakness into strength?

9.4   PROFESSIONAL NETWORK

Employers and hiring managers want employees that would fit into the team and help them to succeed. Thus they depend on referrals from their professional networks, interviews and references for a feel of the candidates that will most closely fit the 'person' on their minds for the role. Put crudely, they want to work with who they are most comfortable with. Yes, the equal opportunity, anti-discrimination laws are there, but the system in the west is not perfect, as expected of any human creation. But how often would a new immigrant stand the chance? Would they be in the network of such hiring managers?

What about the situations with names? Compare 'John' to 'Uwangatugugaga.' Even if many immigrants do not have names as complex, but it is common for them to attach much importance to names and associated cultural affiliations. However, this could become a source of weakness in competing for scarce employment opportunities. What is the first impression on the minds of hiring managers when they see these names?

The reality is that new and emerging immigrants do not have as much professional network that will lead to many potential job opportunities and employers. It takes time to build such a network after the relocation. The saying *your network is your net-worth* also applies to careers.

REMARKS AND GUIDANCE ON HOW TO ADOPT & ADAPT

For new and emerging immigrants: Get out of your comfort zones to meet people and preferably, more locals, strangers and not just staying around people like you. The earlier this is done, the better. Thankfully, the act of networking can be learnt and mastered.

Be open-minded and try not to prejudge, the most viable help could come from unexpected quarters. Display hunger for success and achievements. Be authentic and positive when you talk about your story. Take time to select and put forward your best references for job applications.

REFLECTIONS:

- If you are yet to relocate: what can you do now to turn this weakness into strength?

- Already in the new location: what can you do now to turn this weakness into strength?

10 THREATS

FACTORS IN THE ENVIRONMENT THAT COULD CAUSE TROUBLE FOR YOUR CAREER

> "In the middle of difficulty lies opportunity" *Albert Eistein*

The practical reality of threats would be presented for 3 different contexts – one's personal life, the workplace, and the global environment.

Career is important for income, esteem and wellbeing. Unfortunately, the pursuit of work including efforts at overcoming the barriers presented earlier in this workbook can cause loss of focus on other key aspects of life - personal and family. The resulting imbalance can threaten the ability to achieve the career goals themselves. Many immigrants are caught up in this dilemma. There is need for ongoing balance!

People commonly experience workplace issues including discrimination, bullying, unfair dismissal, etc. These situations have often derailed the careers of newcomers who are mostly unaware of their workplace rights and lack the skill to engage accordingly. Global factors also threaten jobs and careers. Some recent ones are the global financial crisis 2009, the oil price slump 2014-2016, and COVID-19 Pandemic 2020. People of all backgrounds are impacted. However, immigrants are particularly vulnerable due to the factors already highlighted in this book.

REMARKS AND GUIDANCE ON HOW TO ADOPT & ADAPT

Firstly, acknowledge that these situations will happen. There is little you can do to stop their occurrence or hasten them to finish.

Maintain physical, mental and spiritual wellness during such situations. Build a strong friendship and network base for survival and progress.

Build robustness and contingencies into your skillset. Scan the environment for opportunities. Activate different skills, qualifications and networks as the dispensation demands. Educate yourself and be aware of your rights. Exercise them boldly!

REFLECTIONS:

- What lessons have been learnt from the GFC, Oil price slump, COVID-19, etc.?

- Whilst no one can predict, how can these lessons be used to prepare for the future?

PART 4

<hr>

SUSTAINABLE ACHIEVEMENT OF YOUR GOALS!

11 TRACKING PROGRESS & CELEBRATING ACHIEVEMENTS

> "Without deviation from the norm, progress is not possible" *Frank Zappa*

> "Don't mistake activity with achievement" *John Wooden*

> "Life is 10% what happens to you and 90% how you react to it"
> *Charles Swindoll*

What does the definition of successful achievement of your migration and integration goals look like for you? Could it be about securing a high-paying employment or business and generating enough income to care for yourself, your immediate family, your extended family, and still have enough to lead a high quality life at retirement? This should tie back to your set goals and how you are tracking against anticipated progress. However soft it may be, it is vital to be able to confirm and measure actual progress in one form or the other which will be best known to you.

It is wise to celebrate little wins and achievements along the journey of life and particularly as a migrant that has made such a significant move.

REFLECTIONS:

○ How would you track progress against your set migration and integration goals?

○ How would you differentiate between being busy and achievement (being productive)?

○ How would you celebrate your achievements along the way?

12 CONTINUOUS IMPROVEMENT FOR SUSTAINABLE GROWTH

> "What gets measured gets improved" *Peter Drucker*

> "Nothing to prove, everything to improve" *@agentsteven*

More often, things would not proceed exactly as planned regarding achieving your migration and integration goals. The situation will deserve a continuous improvement process as you experience deviations, inevitably. Even when everything seems to be working well in your favour, you will still explore opportunities for improvement. For example, you will be acquiring new skills even if you landed a dream job within a relatively short time of arriving in the new location. The employment and business environment change so quickly and wisdom demands trying to be ahead of the curve.

Conversely, there may be situations where you have not been able to secure a job at all even when you resort to chasing roles that are well below your capabilities, just to get into the market. Again, continuous improvement demand that you keep taking steps to close gaps abd achieve your goals despite taking more time than planned.

REFLECTIONS:

○ How would you ensure continuous improvements when things are going as planned?

○ How would you ensure continuous improvements when things do not go as planned?

RESOURCES

- Written for all ages and cultural backgrounds, this extraordinary story takes about an hour to read, but the insights can last a lifetime.

- When you know the real stories of real people, you can prepare yourself better on how to deal with change in your own journey.

- All stakeholders will find useful hints and tips in reading this book given the increasing need for cultural integration in our schools, workplaces, neighbourhoods and communities

This book presents stories and useful information about:

- The benefits of immigration.
- Learning to succeed despite the odds.
- Practical steps for employment & whole-life.
  You will find if you are:
- An intending or new immigrant.
- A settled immigrant looking for guidance.
- Non-immigrants, international students, government & community leaders – for cultural intelligence.

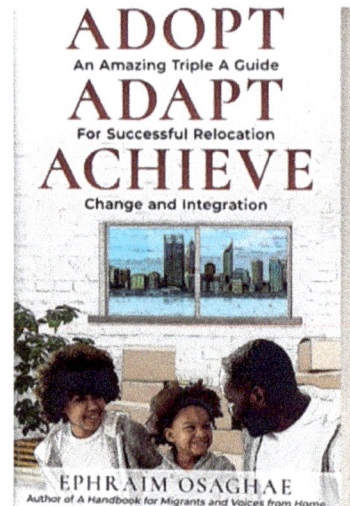

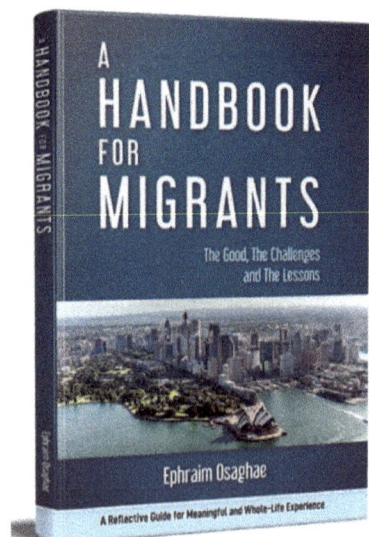

ADOPT
An Amazing Triple A Guide
ADAPT
For Successful Relocation
ACHIEVE
Change and Integration

EPHRAIM OSAGHAE
Author of A Handbook for Migrants and Voices from Home

A
HANDBOOK
FOR
MIGRANTS
The Good, The Challenges
and The Lessons

Ephraim Osaghae

A Reflective Guide for Meaningful and Whole-Life Experience

GET ALL THE BOOKS ON amazon

RESOURCES

VOICES FROM Home

A NARRATION OF PARENTS OF FIRST-GENERATION MIGRANTS

WISDOM FROM OUR DIASPORIC ROOTS

EPHRAIM OSAGHAE MBL

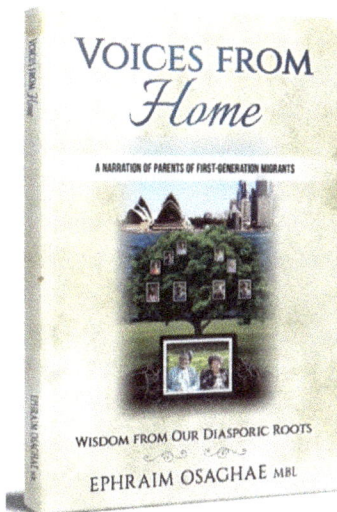

Every human is part of a bigger family with roots that extend beyond places and cultures of current residences. This is true for immigrants and people of multicultural backgrounds. Would it not be beneficial to know and explore the advantages and implications of roots?

- This book provides insights on the key dynamics of cultures, motivations, and family structures.
- It informs global audiences about lived experiences of people of migrant backgrounds.
- It contributes to the conversations on identity, cultural intelligence and sustainable migration.

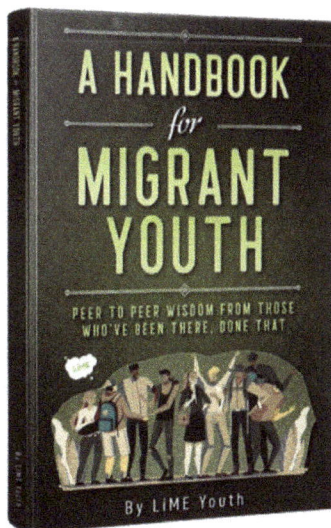

A HANDBOOK for MIGRANT YOUTH

PEER TO PEER WISDOM FROM THOSE WHO'VE BEEN THERE, DONE THAT

By LiME Youth

- Authored by 18 multicultural lime youth from 14 different national backgrounds, this book provides a glimpse into the contemporary world of immigrant youth.

- All young people - migrants and non-migrants - will find the information in this book very useful. Same with parents, mentors, teachers, school administrators and other members of the community.

- Compiled by Ephraim Osaghae

GET ALL THE BOOKS ON amazon